FINGERPICKING Christmas

Introduction to Fingerstyle Guitar 2

Angels We Have Heard on High 3
Away in a Manger 6
Deck the Hall 8
The First Noël 10
Go, Tell It on the Mountain 12
God Rest Ye Merry, Gentlemen 14
Good King Wenceslas 16
Hark! The Herald Angels Sing 18
I Saw Three Ships 7
It Came Upon the Midnight Clear 20
Jingle Bells 22
Joy to the World 24
O Christmas Tree 26
O Come, All Ye Faithful (Adeste Fideles) 28
O Little Town of Bethlehem 30
Silent Night 32
Up on the Housetop 34
We Three Kings of Orient Are 36
We Wish You a Merry Christmas 40
What Child Is This? 38

ISBN 978-0-634-06247-6

Copyright © 2003 by HAL LEONARD CORPORATION
International Copyright Secured All Rights Reserved

For all works contained herein:
Unauthorized copying, arranging, adapting, recording
or public performance is an infringement of copyright.
Infringers are liable under the law.

Visit Hal Leonard Online at www.halleonard.com

HAL•LEONARD® CORPORATION
7777 W. Bluemound Rd. P.O. Box 13819 Milwaukee, WI 53213

INTRODUCTION TO FINGERSTYLE GUITAR

Fingerstyle (a.k.a. fingerpicking) is a guitar technique that means you literally pick the strings with your right-hand fingers and thumb. This contrasts with the conventional technique of strumming and playing single notes with a pick (a.k.a. flatpicking). For fingerpicking, you can use any type of guitar: acoustic steel-string, nylon-string classical, or electric.

THE RIGHT HAND

The most common right-hand position is shown here.

Use a high wrist; arch your palm as if you were holding a ping-pong ball. Keep the thumb outside and away from the fingers, and let the fingers do the work rather than lifting your whole hand.

The thumb generally plucks the bottom strings with downstrokes on the left side of the thumb and thumbnail. The other fingers pluck the higher strings using upstrokes with the fleshy tip of the fingers and fingernails. The thumb and fingers should pluck one string per stroke and not brush over several strings.

Another picking option you may choose to use is called hybrid picking (a.k.a. plectrum-style fingerpicking). Here, the pick is usually held between the thumb and first finger, and the three remaining fingers are assigned to pluck the higher strings.

THE LEFT HAND

The left-hand fingers are numbered 1 through 4.

Be sure to keep your fingers arched, with each joint bent; if they flatten out across the strings, they will deaden the sound when you fingerpick. As a general rule, let the strings ring as long as possible when playing fingerstyle.

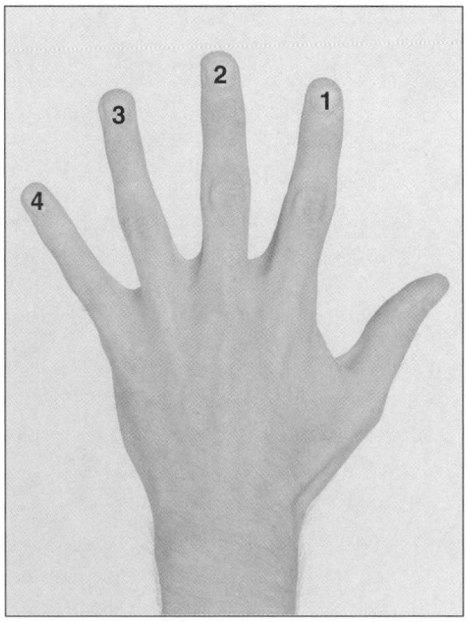

Angels We Have Heard on High

Traditional French Carol
Translated by James Chadwick

Copyright © 2003 by HAL LEONARD CORPORATION
International Copyright Secured All Rights Reserved

Chorus
C Am Dm G
Glo - -
C F G
- ri - a
Am G C Dm C G
in ex - cel - sis De - o.
C Am Dm G
Glo - -

Additional Lyrics

3. Come to Bethlehem and see
Him whose birth the angels sing;
Come adore on bended knee
Christ the Lord, the newborn King.

4. See within a manger laid
Jesus, Lord of heaven and earth!
Mary, Joseph, lend your aid,
With us sing our Savior's birth.

Away in a Manger

Traditional
Words by John T. McFarland (v.3)
Music by James R. Murray

Copyright © 2003 by HAL LEONARD CORPORATION
International Copyright Secured All Rights Reserved

I Saw Three Ships

Traditional English Carol

Additional Lyrics

4. Pray, whither sailed those ships all three?
5. O, they sailed into Bethlehem.
6. And all the bells on earth shall ring,
7. And all the angels in heaven sing,
8. And all the souls on earth shall sing,
9. Then let us all rejoice again!

Copyright © 2003 by HAL LEONARD CORPORATION
International Copyright Secured All Rights Reserved

Deck the Hall

Traditional Welsh Carol

Copyright © 2003 by HAL LEONARD CORPORATION
International Copyright Secured All Rights Reserved

G7 C G Em D
Don we now our gay ap - par - el; fa, la, la, la, la, la,
Fol - low me in mer - ry mea - sure; fa, la, la, la, la, la,
Sing we joy - ous, all to - geth - er; fa, la, la, la, la, la,

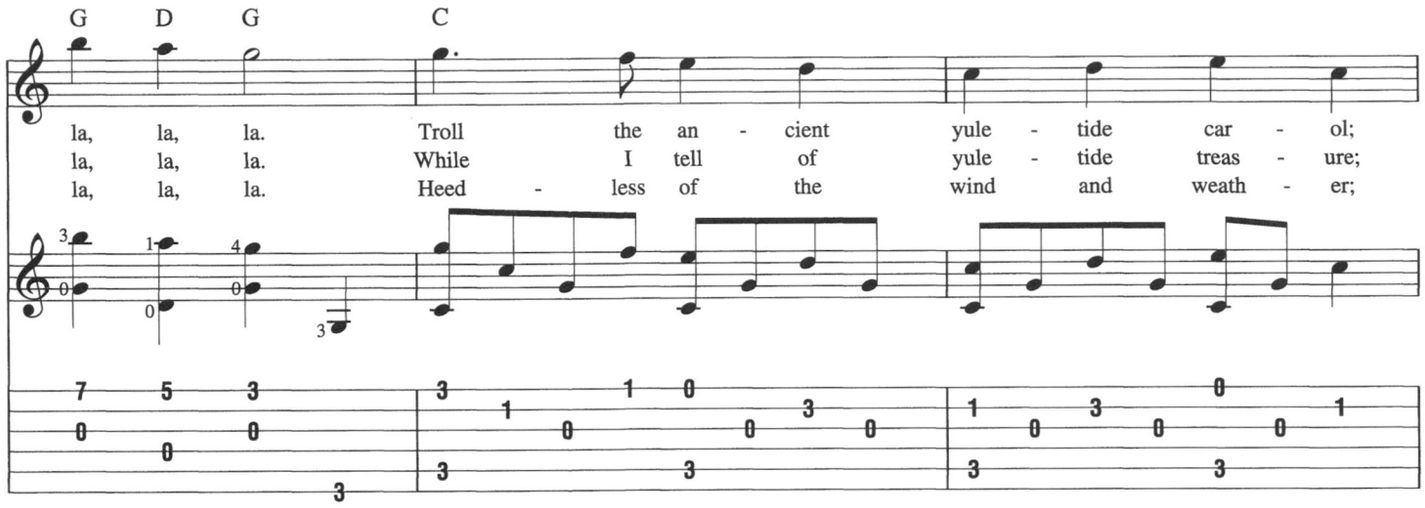
G D G C
la, la, la. Troll the an - cient yule - tide car - ol;
la, la, la. While I tell of yule - tide treas - ure;
la, la, la. Heed - less of the wind and weath - er;

1., 2.
3.
F C G C G C
fa, la, la, la, la, la, la, la, la. la, la, la.
fa, la, la, la, la, la, la, la, la.
fa, la, la, la, la, la,

The First Noël

17th Century English Carol
Music from W. Sandys' Christmas Carols

Copyright © 2003 by HAL LEONARD CORPORATION
International Copyright Secured All Rights Reserved

Additional Lyrics

4. This star drew nigh to the northwest,
O'er Bethlehem it took its rest;
And there it did both stop and stay,
Right over the place where Jesus lay.

5. Then entered in those wise men three,
Full reverently upon the knee;
And offered there His presence,
Their gold, and myrrh, and frankincense.

6. Then let us all with one accord
Sing praises to our heav'nly Lord;
That hath made heav'n and earth of naught,
And with His blood mankind hath bought.

Go, Tell It on the Mountain

African-American Spiritual
Verses by John W. Work, Jr.

Copyright © 2003 by HAL LEONARD CORPORATION
International Copyright Secured All Rights Reserved

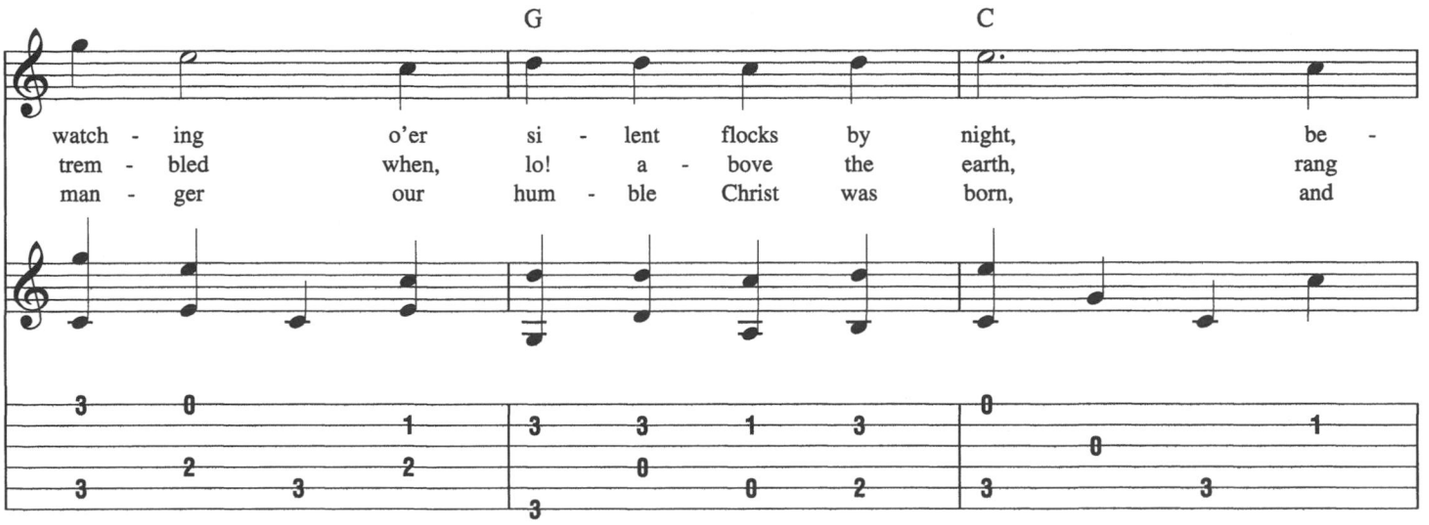
G
C
watch - ing o'er si - lent flocks by night, be -
trem - bled when, lo! a - bove the earth, rang
man - ger our hum - ble Christ was born, and

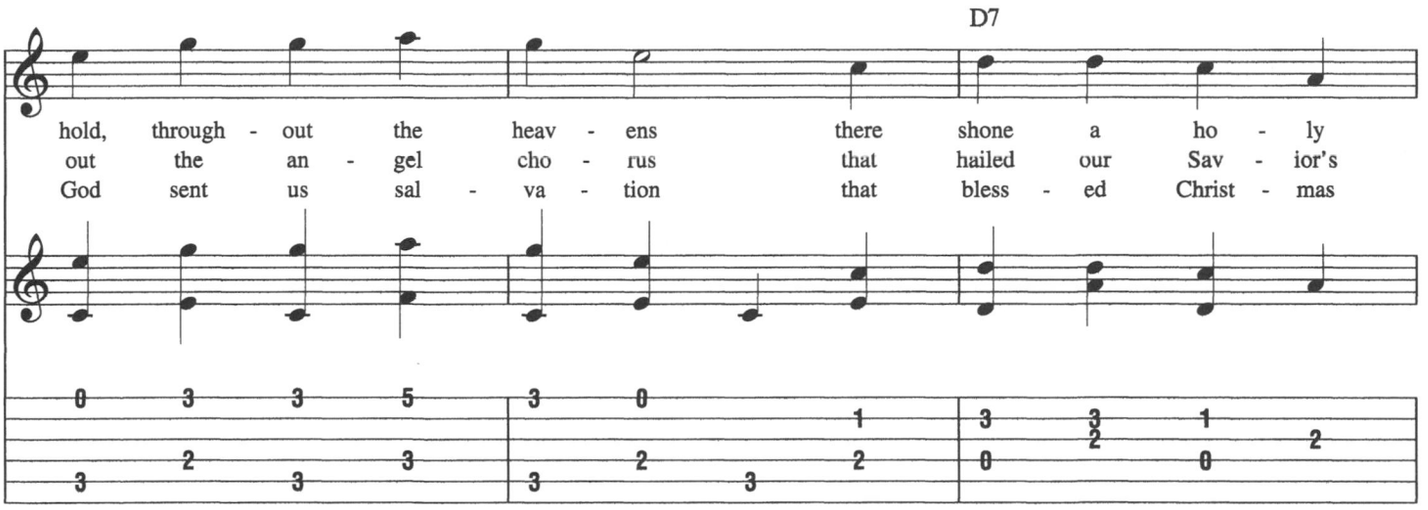
D7
hold, through - out the heav - ens there shone a ho - ly
out the an - gel cho - rus that hailed our Sav - ior's
God sent us sal - va - tion that bless - ed Christ - mas

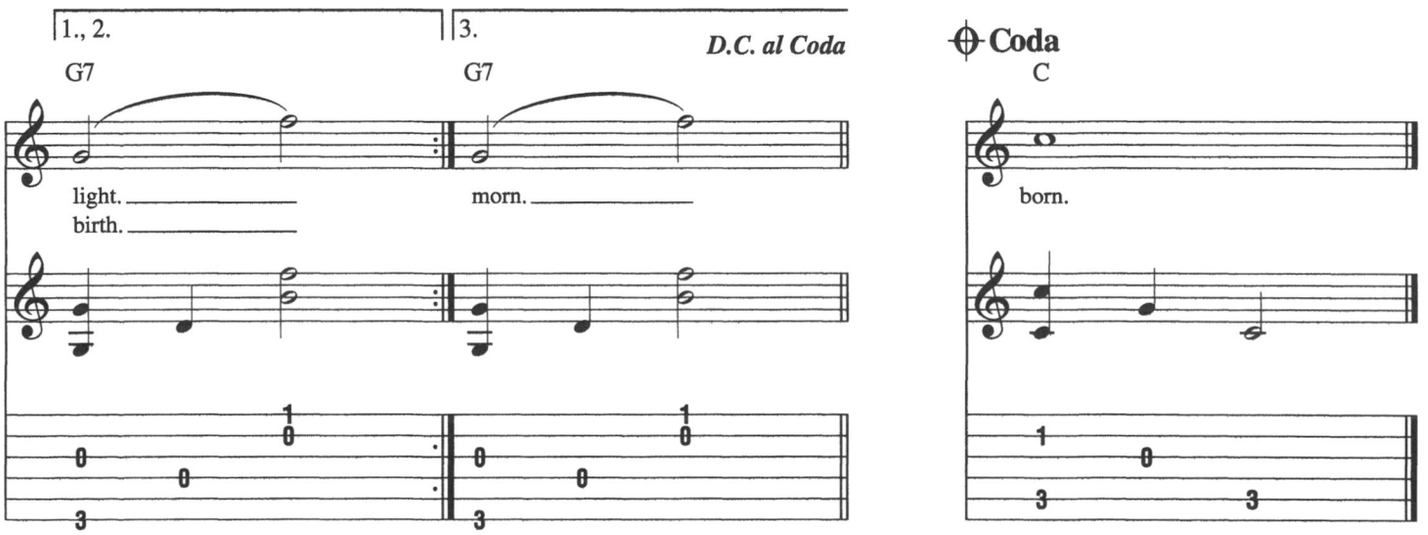
1., 2.
3.
D.C. al Coda
Coda
G7
G7
C
light.
birth.
morn.
born.

God Rest Ye Merry, Gentlmen

19th Century English Carol

Copyright © 2003 by HAL LEONARD CORPORATION
International Copyright Secured All Rights Reserved

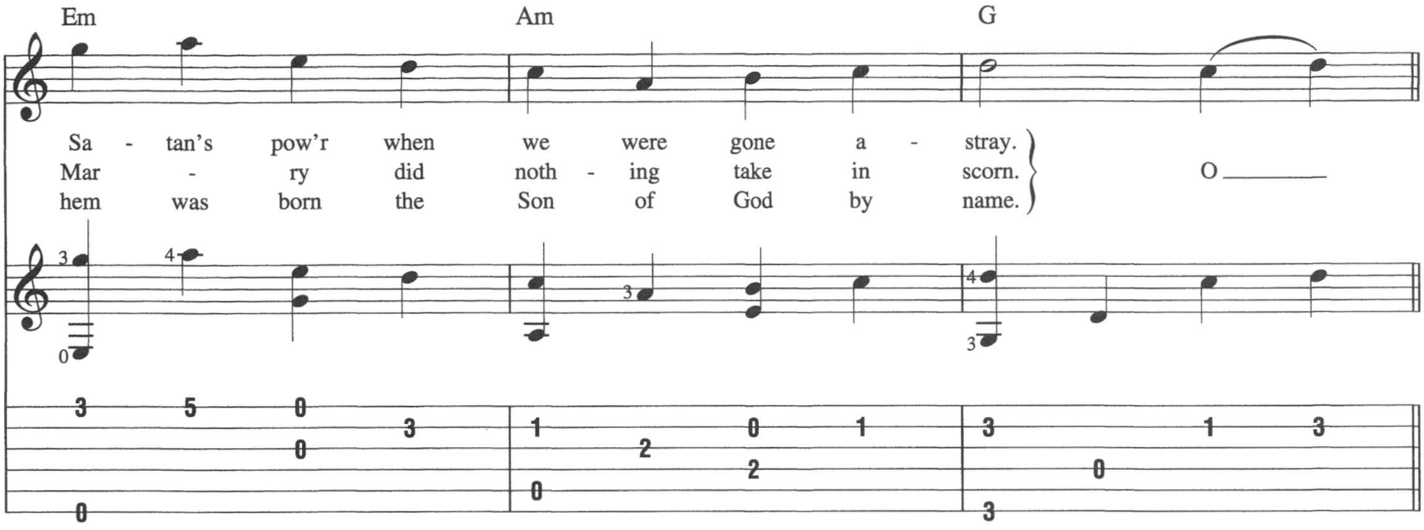
Em
Am
G
Sa - tan's pow'r when we were gone a - stray.
Mar - ry did noth - ing take in scorn.
hem was born the Son of God by name.
O

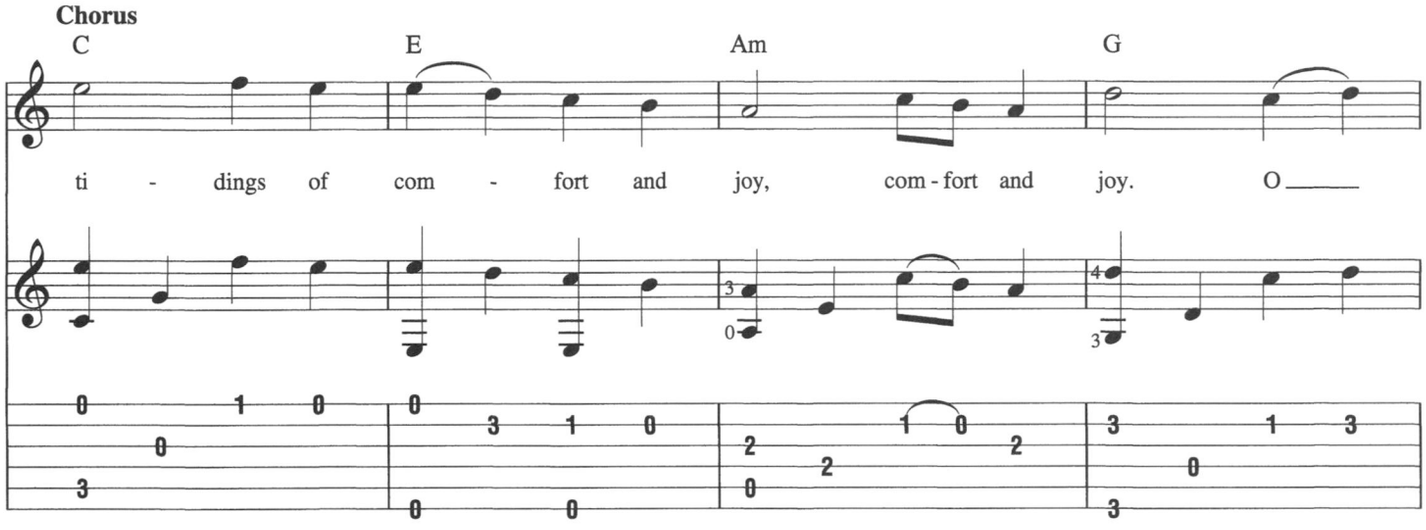
Chorus
C
E
Am
G
ti - dings of com - fort and joy, com - fort and joy. O

C
E
1., 2.
Am
3.
Am
ti - dings of com - fort and joy! 2. In joy!
3. From

Good King Wenceslas

Words by John M. Neale
Music from Piae Cantiones

Copyright © 2003 by HAL LEONARD CORPORATION
International Copyright Secured All Rights Reserved

Additional Lyrics

4. "Sire, the night is darker now,
And the wind blows stronger;
Fails my heart, I know not how,
I can go not longer."
"Mark my footsteps, my good page,
Tread thou in them boldly:
Thou shalt find the winter's rage
Freeze thy blood less coldly."

5. In his master's steps he trod,
Where the snow lay dinted;
Heat was in the very sod
Which the saint has printed.
Therefore, Christian men, be sure,
Wealth or rank possessing;
Ye who now will bless the poor,
Shall yourselves find blessing.

Hark! The Herald Angels Sing

Words by Charles Wesley
Altered by George Whitefield
Music by Felix Mendelssohn-Bartholdy
Arranged by William H. Cummings

Copyright © 2003 by HAL LEONARD CORPORATION
International Copyright Secured All Rights Reserved

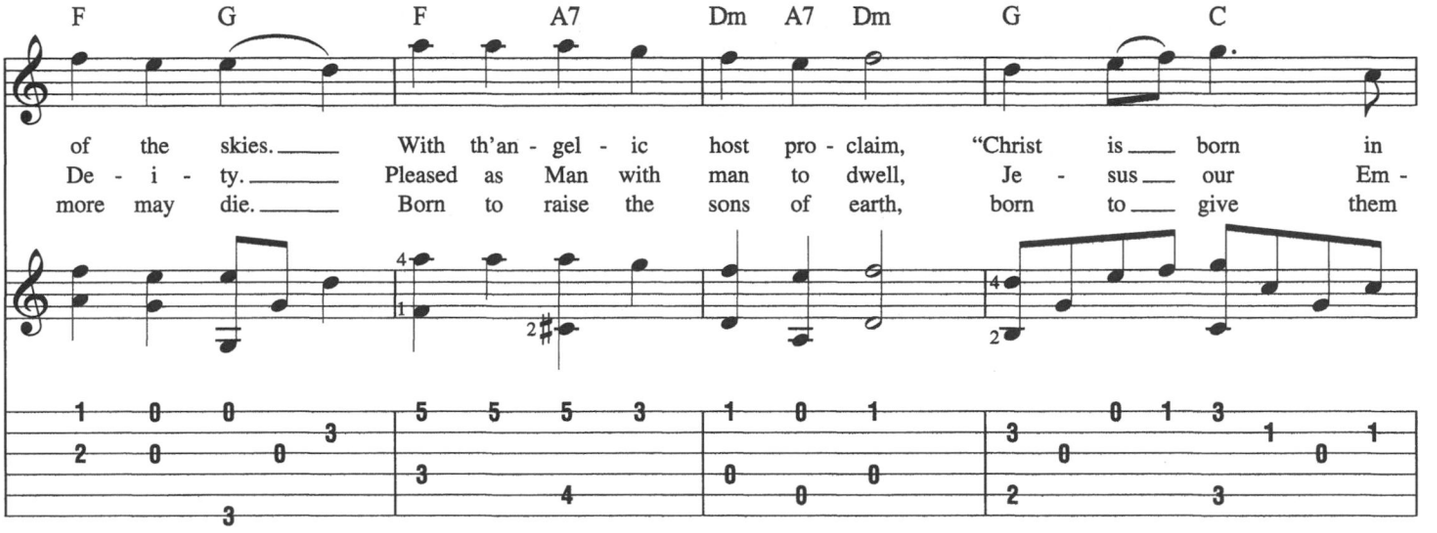
F G F A7 Dm A7 Dm G C
of the skies. With th'an - gel - ic host pro - claim, "Christ is born in
De - i - ty. Pleased as Man with man to dwell, Je - sus our Em -
more may die. Born to raise the sons of earth, born to give them

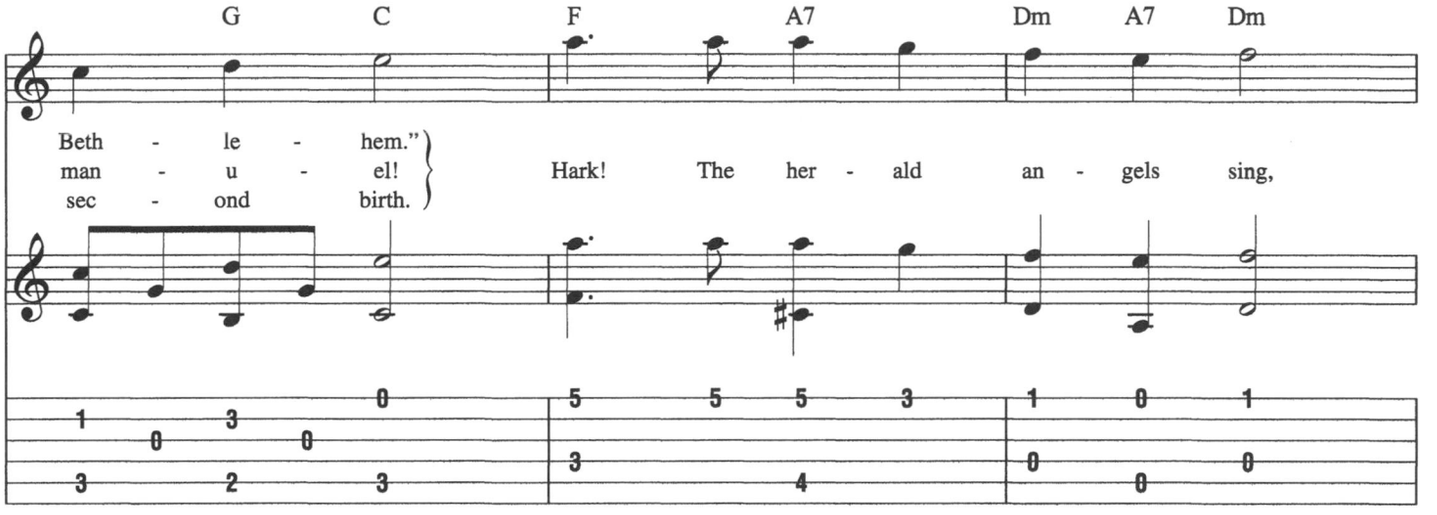
G C F A7 Dm A7 Dm
Beth - le - hem."
man - u - el!
sec - ond birth.
Hark! The her - ald an - gels sing,

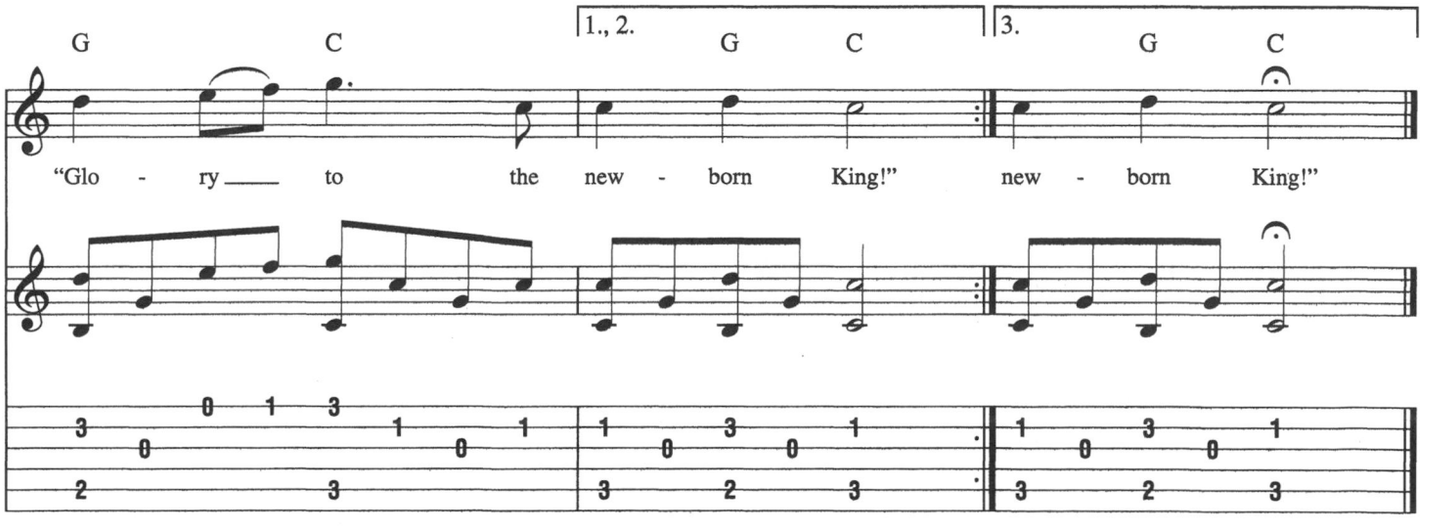
G C 1., 2. G C 3. G C
"Glo - ry to the new - born King!" new - born King!"

It Came Upon the Midnight Clear

Words by Edmund H. Sears
Traditional English Melody
Adapted by Arthur Sullivan

Copyright © 2003 by HAL LEONARD CORPORATION
International Copyright Secured All Rights Reserved

E
Am
G
on the earth, good will to men, from heav - ven's all -

D7
G
C
F
gra - cious King." The world in sol - emn

C
F
G
C
still - ness lay to hear the an - gels sing.

Jingle Bells

Words and Music by J. Pierpont

Copyright © 2003 by HAL LEONARD CORPORATION
International Copyright Secured All Rights Reserved

Chorus
C G C
sleigh - ing song to - night! Oh!
we, we got up - shot! Oh!
crack, you'll take the lead! Oh!
Jin - gle bells, jin - gle bells, jin - gle all the
F C D7
way. Oh, what fun it is to ride in a one horse o - pen
G C
sleigh! Jin - gle bells, jin - gle bells, jin - gle all the way.
F C G C C
1., 2. 3.
Oh, what fun it is to ride in a one horse o - pen sleigh! 2. A sleigh!

Joy to the World

Words by Isaac Watts
Music by George Frideric Handel

Copyright © 2003 by HAL LEONARD CORPORATION
International Copyright Secured All Rights Reserved

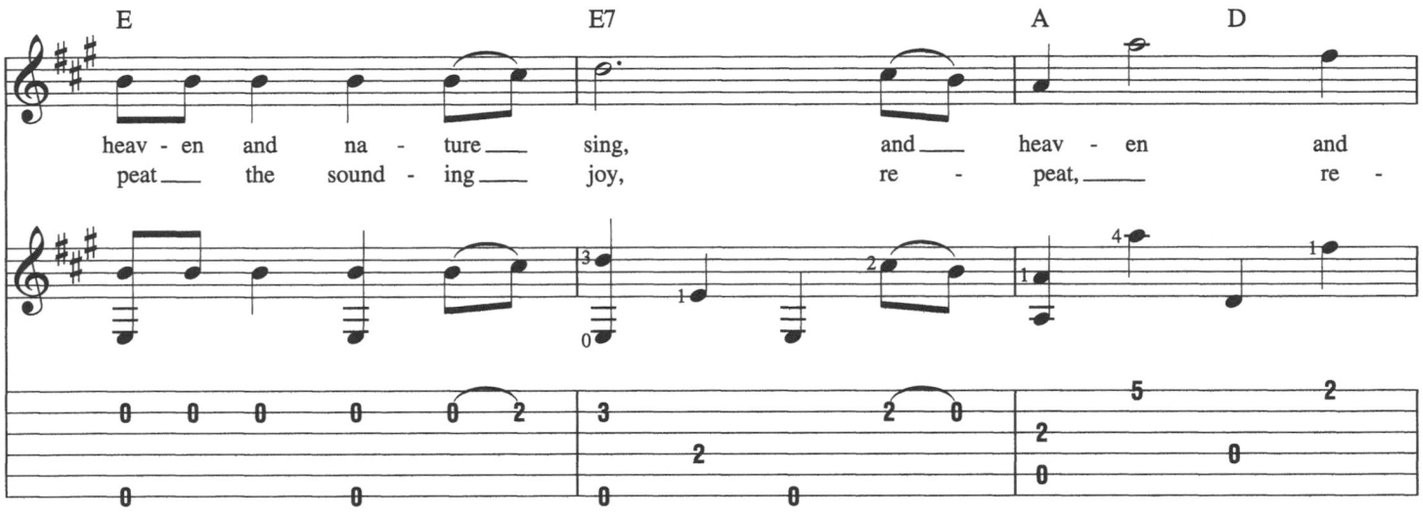

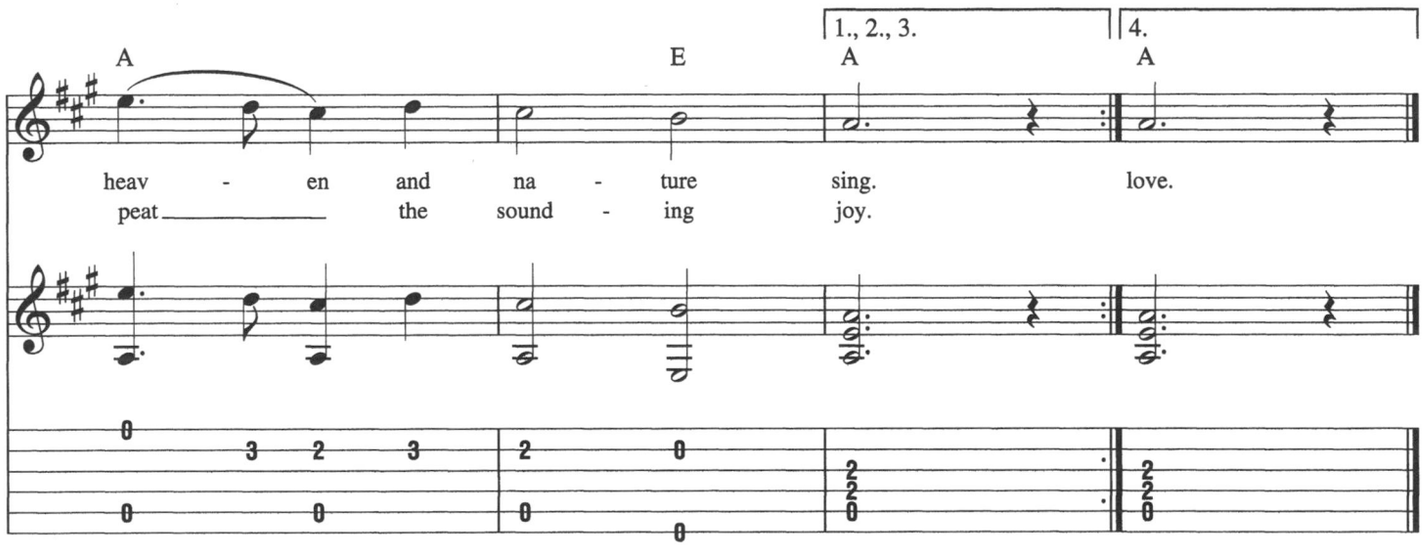

Additional Lyrics

3. No more let sin, and sorrow grow,
Nor thorns infest the ground;
He comes to make His blessings flow
Far as the curse is found,
Far as the curse is found,
Far as, far as the curse is found.

4. He rules the world with truth and grace,
And makes the nations prove
The glories of His righteousness,
And wonders of His love,
And wonders of His love,
And wonders, wonders of His love.

O Christmas Tree

Traditional German Carol

Copyright © 2003 by HAL LEONARD CORPORATION
International Copyright Secured All Rights Reserved

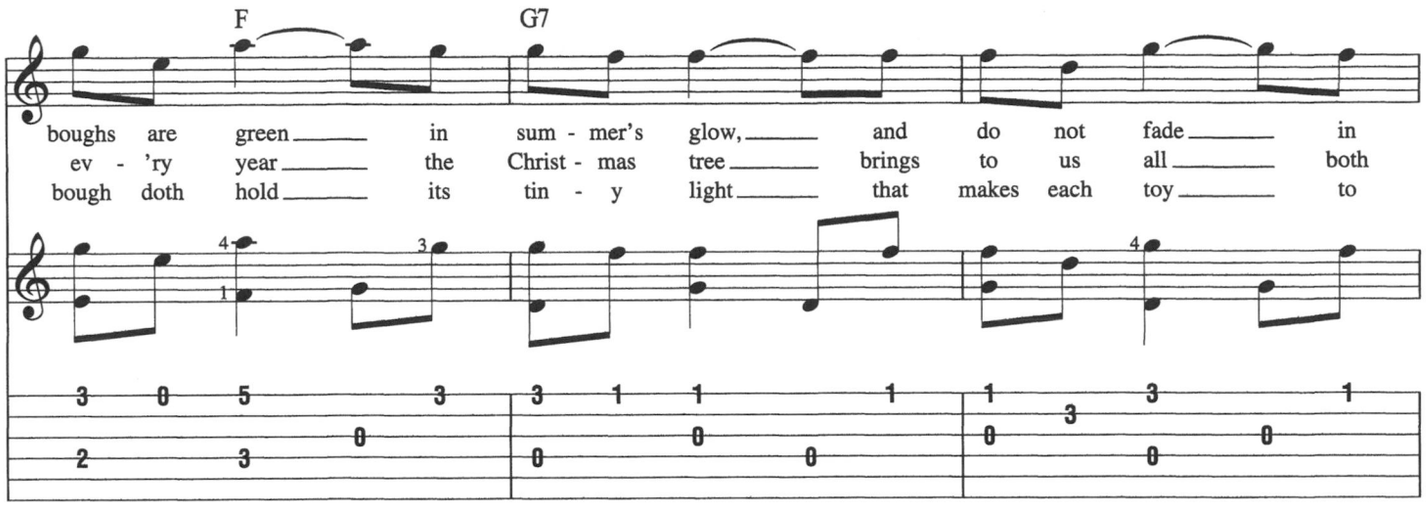
F G7
boughs are green in sum - mer's glow, and do not fade in
ev - 'ry year the Christ - mas tree brings to us all both
bough doth hold its tin - y light that makes each toy to

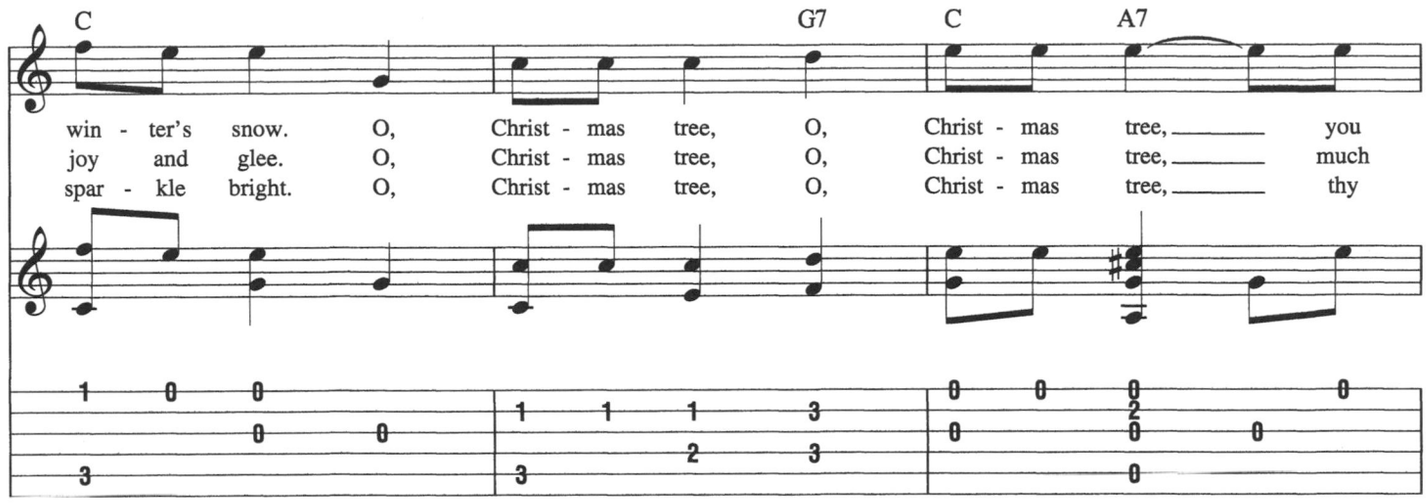
C G7 C A7
win - ter's snow. O, Christ - mas tree, O, Christ - mas tree, you
joy and glee. O, Christ - mas tree, O, Christ - mas tree, much
spar - kle bright. O, Christ - mas tree, O, Christ - mas tree, thy

1., 2. 3.
Dm G C G G7 C
stand in ver - dant beau - ty! 2. O, bright - ly!
pleas - ure doth thou bring me! 3. O,
can - dles shine out

O Come, All Ye Faithful

(Adeste Fideles)

Words and Music by John Francis Wade
Latin Words translated by Frederick Oakeley

Copyright © 2003 by HAL LEONARD CORPORATION
International Copyright Secured All Rights Reserved

Chorus
G C G C G C
an - gels.
high - est.
pear - ing.
O come, let us a - dore Him. O
G C Dm C G C Dm C G Am
come, let us a - dore Him. O come, let us a -
G F C G C C
1., 2.
3.
dore Him, Christ, the Lord! Lord!

O Little Town of Bethlehem

Words by Phillips Brooks
Music by Lewis H. Redner

Copyright © 2003 by HAL LEONARD CORPORATION
International Copyright Secured All Rights Reserved

Dm E Am
in the dark streets shin - eth the ev - er - last - ing
morn - ing stars, to - geth - er pro - claim the ho - ly
E C Dm
light; the hopes and fears of all the years are
birth! And prais - es sing to God the King, and
C G C C
1. 2.
met in thee to - night. 2. For earth!
peace to men on

Silent Night

Words by Joseph Mohr
Translated by John F. Young
Music by Franz X. Gruber

Copyright © 2003 by HAL LEONARD CORPORATION
International Copyright Secured All Rights Reserved

C
G
Ho - ly in - fant so ten - der and mild.
Heav - 'nly hosts sing al - le - lu - ia.
with the dawn of re - deem - ing grace.

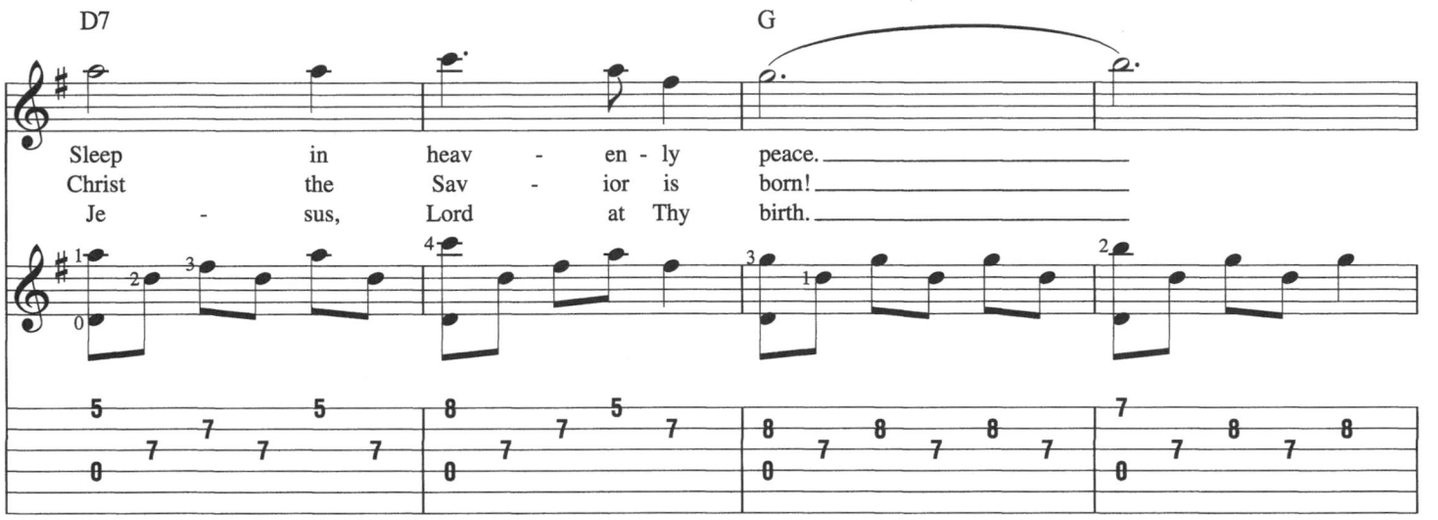
D7
G
Sleep in heav - en - ly peace.
Christ the Sav - ior is born!
Je - sus, Lord at Thy birth.

D7
G
1., 2.
3.
Sleep in heav - en - ly peace.
Christ the Sav - ior is born!
Je - sus, Lord at Thy birth.

Up on the Housetop

Words and Music by B.R. Handy

Copyright © 2003 by HAL LEONARD CORPORATION
International Copyright Secured All Rights Reserved

Chorus
C
G
D7
Ho, ho, ho, who would - n't go? Ho, ho, ho,
G
C
who would - n't go? Up on the house - top, click, click, click.
G
1., 2.
D
G
3.
D
G
Down through the chim - ney with good Saint Nick. good Saint Nick.

We Three Kings of Orient Are

Words and Music by John H. Hopkins, Jr.

Copyright © 2003 by HAL LEONARD CORPORATION
International Copyright Secured All Rights Reserved

Additional Lyrics

4. Myrrh is mine: its bitter perfume
Breathes a life of gathering gloom.
Sorrowing, sighing, bleeding, dying;
Sealed in the stone-cold tomb.

5. Glorious now, behold Him arise,
King and God, and Sacrifice!
Heav'n sings alleluia,
Alleluia, the earth replies:

What Child Is This?

Words by William C. Dix
16th Century English Melody

Copyright © 2003 by HAL LEONARD CORPORATION
International Copyright Secured All Rights Reserved

C G Em Am
ing? This, this is Christ the King, whom shep - herds
ing. Nails, spear, shall pierce Him through, the cross be
Him. Raise, raise your song on high while Mar - y

E C G
guard and an - gels sing: Haste, haste to bring him
borne for me and you. Hail, hail the Sav - iour
sings a lul - la - by. Joy, joy for Christ is

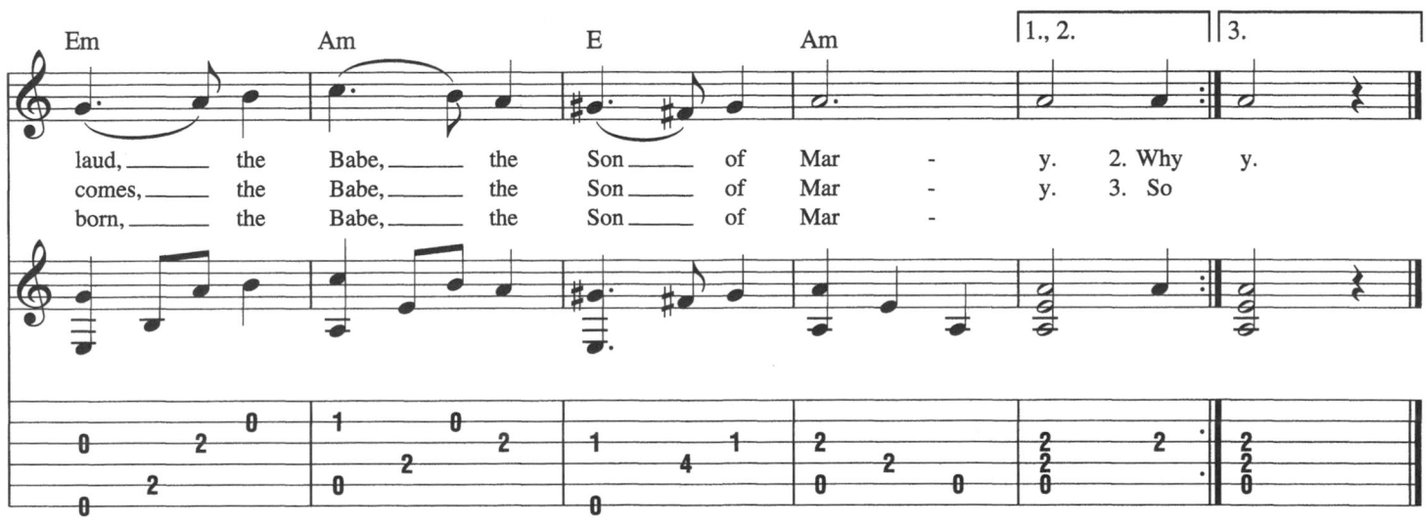
Em Am E Am
1., 2. 3.
laud, the Babe, the Son of Mar - y. 2. Why y.
comes, the Babe, the Son of Mar - y. 3. So
born, the Babe, the Son of Mar -

We Wish You a Merry Christmas

Traditional English Folksong

Copyright © 2003 by HAL LEONARD CORPORATION
International Copyright Secured All Rights Reserved